Cultural Awakenings

Immersive Insights into Global Traditions

Table of Contents

Culture is the widening of the mind and of the
spirit.

Chapter 1. Introduction

Step into a panorama of vibrant colors, sounds, and textures with our Special Report: "Cultural Awakenings: Immersive Insights into Global Traditions." Discover the richness of diverse cultures that stitch the fabric of our collective human heritage. This captivating journey is not confined to geographical boundaries or set timelines; instead, it spans across continents, soars over centuries, and dives deep into socio-cultural bedrock to celebrate global traditions at their most authentic. Engage with captivating stories, delve into unique artistic expressions, and unearth the roots of age-old customs. You won't just be observing - you'll be immersing! Let this special report be your passport to an expansive world of cultural exploration - a guaranteed page-turner you'll want to add to your collection today!

Chapter 2. Unveiling the Bedrock: The Genesis of Tradition

As our exploration commences, we delve deep into the roots of human existence, where rituals and traditions were born, molded by time, society, and human perception. Understanding the genesis of tradition marks the starting point of our cultural awakening. Herein lie the seeds of human civilization, sown by our ancestors, and nurtured by their convictions, values, and experiences.

2.1. The Dawn of Traditions: A Paleolithic Perspective

Our journey into our collective past begins with the dawn of the Paleolithic era, tracing back approximately 2.5 million years. The Paleolithic period was not just a time of significant biological evolution but it also marked the emergence of early human cultures and traditions. The very first traditions can be identified in the Paleolithic hunters and gatherers who created stone tools. The repetitive, standardized nature of these tools points towards the existence of 'traditions' - ways of doing things passed down from one generation to the next.

The stone tool making tradition marked the advent of cultural transmission through imitation and learning, setting the stage for more complex traditions in the epochs to follow. The Paleolithic culture also indicated the early development of sacred traditions and rituals, as seen from the discovery of animal and human figurines indicative of spiritual and religious practices.

2.2. Neolithic Revolution: The Cradle of Civilization

The Neolithic Revolution, occurring around ten thousand years ago, molded a crucial chapter in the genesis of tradition. During this period, humans made the significant transition from nomadic hunter-gatherer societies to more settled, agrarian communities. This transition itself was a tradition-enabler, providing the structure and stability that allowed cultural practices to flourish.

The birth of agriculture played a crucial role in the development of traditions, particularly those linked to the agricultural calendar. Alongside this, the settled nature of these communities spawned a wide array of artisanal traditions through pottery, weaving, and metalworking. The belief systems also evolved, potent with deities of fertility, earth, and agricultural cycles, which subsequently brought about the birth of religious practices and rituals.

2.3. Bronze Age and Iron Age: Tradition in Metallurgy

Following the Neolithic era, the Bronze Age and Iron Age showcased a profound transformation in human society and traditions, primarily driven by advancements in metalworking. Craftsmanship traditions revolving around bronze and iron became pivotal. These metals weren't just tools, they were symbols of society's hierarchy, thereby adding social and symbolic dimensions to the act of craftsmanship.

Bronze and iron tools and artifacts found at archaeological sites across varied geographies point towards sophistication in techniques, further indicating the 'teaching and learning' construct of transferring these skills across generations. Much like the previous eras, the traditions of this period, too, were extensively influenced by prevailing belief systems, techniques of warfare, and modes of production.

2.4. Classical Era: Philosophical Traditions as Bedrock

As we move forward in time, the Classical Era emerges as a prominent period in the genesis of what we now consider 'traditional'. Much of this period was characterized by the emergence of philosophical traditions. The philosophies of ancient Greece and India serve as monumental instances of such developments.

In ancient Greece, schools of thought such as Stoicism and Epicureanism germinated, guiding societal norms and values, thus evolving into traditions. Meanwhile, in ancient India, philosophical systems such as Vedanta and Samkhya played similar roles, giving rise to diverse concepts and traditions that pervade Indian culture to this day.

2.5. The Inception of Modern Traditions

Exiting the timeline of epochs, we now move towards more recent history. The Middle Ages, Renaissance, Industrial Revolution, and post-modern era, albeit diverse, boasted their unique traditions, further paving the way for modern customs. These periods saw the evolution of architecture, music, painting, literature, and more manifesting into traditions that not only reflected but also shaped societies.

Times of significant transformation - like the Enlightenment and the Industrial Revolution - dramatically altered societal values and ways of life, thereby creating new traditions by displacing and modifying older ones. The evolution of institutions such as marriage, for example, has seen immense shifts due to such periods of change. What were once considered 'traditional' roles and norms within the institution has been redefined, underlining the malleable nature of traditions.

This panoramic chronicle of the genesis of tradition underscores the intrinsic link between tradition and the society from which it emanates. The insight it provides is both humbling and enlightening, serving as the bedrock from which we begin to understand the complexity and richness of the culture conquered in the following chapters. Steeped in history and human experience, traditions provide a looking glass into societal evolution marked not just by time, but also by the continually metamorphosing human collective consciousness.

Chapter 3. Art as Reflections: Global Expressions of Culture

The exploration painting the panorama of cultural insights embarks upon the realm of art with this chapter. A deep understanding of art invariably requires an in-depth introspection into its myriad forms. Extending across the globe, each one whispers a different tale - dictated by heritage, nurtured by history, and flourishing in their unique cultural contexts.

3.1. The Dawn of Artistic Endeavors

The dawn of artistic endeavors lies buried within the age-old annals of human history. If one was to travel back in time to the Paleolithic Age - around 30,000 BCE, archeological evidence reveals that our ancestors breathed life into creations using rudimentary but effective tools. Perfectly imperfect, nascent yet nuanced, they vividly expressed myriad facets of their existence on earthen canvases, cementing the very foundation of artistic expression.

In caves nestled in the depths of time, like those in Lascaux, France, or Altamira, Spain, humanity glimpsed the earliest fragments of art: enigmatic figures of animals — archaic echoes in ochre and charcoal, testifying to our yearning for expression and connection.

3.2. An Odyssey Through Time

Over centuries, art evolved as civilizations flourished, absorbing and reflecting the milieu of its times and harnessing the power of expanding mediums—be it mural painting in ancient Egypt, scroll paintings in China, or mosaic art in ancient Rome.

Art's transformative journey continued through the Middle Ages, further gaining momentum in the Renaissance. The latter heralded a rebirth, with artists like Michelangelo and Da Vinci leaving indelible impressions that still resonate. To journeys in Baroque, Romanticism, Impressionism, art witnessed continual expansion of ingenuity.

Artists reached deeper into their emotional intellect, using brushstrokes and palettes to mirror existential angst, societal turmoil, love, despair, and human resilience. Van Gogh's 'Starry Night' and Edvard Munch's 'The Scream' express a dire intensity of emotion, translating into a form that transcends language barriers and touches raw nerves of universal sentiments.

3.3. An Explosion of Changing Styles and Movements

The journey into the twentieth century saw an explosion of styles, genres, and movements, driven by socio-political change, industrialization, and changing cultural paradigms.

Modernism, Surrealism, Cubism, Expressionism, Pop Art, and Street Art, with creators like Picasso, Salvador Dalí, Andy Warhol, and Banksy, highlighted societies' tangible and intangible facets. Art began challenging conventions, shattering boundaries, and fearlessly delving into the conscious, subconscious, and unconscious mind. Art became a mirror, reflector, and interpreter of the human condition.

3.4. Traditional Art Forms - A Deep Dive into Culture

Reverberating with the pulse of the ancient, traditional art forms are the cultural repositories of communities worldwide. These art forms are imbued with value systems, worldviews, and communal spiritual connections, camouflaging as aesthetic expressions.

Sacred Aboriginal 'Dot Art' in Australia, glorious Madhubani paintings from India, the graceful art of Japanese 'Origami', African tribal masks, the vivid Byzantine mosaics - each reflects their civilization's ethos, narrating tales of their ancestors and preserving cultural wisdom for future generations.

3.5. Art Today: Melting Pot of Global Expressions

Navigating the contemporary artistic landscape is akin to traversing a labyrinth of multi-cultural expressions. Today, confluence of cultures, technological innovations, and new mediums are transforming the canvas of artistic narratives. Digital art, concept art, installation art, virtual reality art, the list is ever-growing and ever-evolving.

Artists like Yayoi Kusama, Ai Weiwei, Olafur Eliasson, or Banksy, each offer a different vantage point, challenge norms, and prompt discourse on myriad themes - be it social justice, existentialism, climate change, identity, or beauty.

Every piece of art is an innovative snapshot – an encapsulation of a moment, an ideation, a dialogue between the artist and the observer, a cultural commentary that needs no translation.

The vibrant world of art demonstrates how human imagination, when fueled by cultural currents, delves into depths hitherto unexplored, recreates realms unseen, and gives birth to universes unparalleled. As the journey through the annals of artistic expressions comes to a pause, remember that each culture's art forms are like a prism – multi-faceted, enigmatic, and waiting to be explored, understood, and appreciated in the world's cultural tapestry.

Chapter 4. Rituals Revelations: The Power of Tradition

To unfurl the power of tradition, we'll touch down upon the vibrant world of rituals, an arena teeming with fascinating customs, collective volition, and symbolic potency. Our exploration revolves around three distinctive themes- ritual's construct, their transcendence through time, and the silent undercurrent that fuels their existence and sustains them in contemporary times and future scenarios.

4.1. Understanding Rituals: The Fabric of Shared Beliefs

Rituals aren't merely actions, but profound expressions of shared beliefs and values that stand as testament to the cultural legacy of a community. They can range from the daily tea ceremony in Japan, the tranquil art of making matcha woven into a choreographed mindfulness exercise- to the vibrant colors of India's Holi, where powdered pigments tossed in the air become a symphony of unity and joyous abandon. Rituals offer a platform for expression, and through them, we connect with our past and project our identity into the future.

Then, there are rituals like the Maasai's coming-of-age ceremony in Kenya, where young men leap into adulthood under the approving gaze of their community, or the respectful harmony between humans and serpents in the 'Nag Panchami' festival in India, highlighting our intricate and sustained relationship with the natural world around us. These rituals embrace the transformative power that traditions have in shaping individual and communal identities over time.

4.2. Time Transcendence: Rituals as Vanguards of Traditions

Peeping through the prism of time, rituals have evolved, adapted, and endured. They resonate with an unfading strength, binding generations together and upholding the torch of culture. Seemingly simple and ordinary acts like a Thanksgiving meal, the Spanish 'Sobremesa' (post-meal conversations), or the Chinese Lunar New Year family feast are imbued with a sense of history, camaraderie, and hearty narratives that supersede their immediate context, offering an intimate lens to observe and appreciate family ties and cultural continuity.

Major global events, such as the Mexican 'Dia de los Muertos' or 'Day of the Dead' and 'Ancestors Day' or 'Qing Ming' in China, stress the importance of ancestral veneration, underscoring the cyclical nature of life and death. Here, the past intertwines with the present, creating a time-transcending continuum where history, sentiment, and an array of vibrant traditions coalesce. Moments turn into millennia; personal memories mingle with collective mythology.

4.3. The Undercurrent: The Power and Purpose of Rituals

Beneath the surface-level spectacle and charisma that rituals often embody, they serve pivotal roles, often conveying important teachings, values or socio-cultural frameworks. Subsequently, they foster a sense of belonging, embedding individuals within a larger framework of shared understanding and communal existence.

Supporting communal harmony, they provide stability during periods of social flux or personal change. An exemplar can be found in Jewish traditions like Bar Mitzvah or Bat Mitzvah, marking the transition to adulthood with a sense of responsibility and religious commitment.

Moreover, rituals like the Native American potlatch, which involve giving away or destroying wealth to uphold a reputation, emphasize a value system grounded in generosity and social prestige, challenging our understanding of wealth, status, and power.

4.4. Rituals Unveiled: The Blossoming into The Future

While steeped in history, rituals aren't immutable. They sway, flex, and shift, on a constant pilgrimage between innovation and preservation. Just as Japan's meticulous tea ceremony borrowed elements from Zen Buddhism over centuries, modern day rituals, too, continue to incorporate influences from advancing technology, transforming socio-economic matrices, & global interconnections, ensuring their relevance & resonance with contemporary times.

In essence, rituals allow us to navigate life's complexities and uncertainties, imparting a rhythm and structure that lend cultural significance and personal meaning. They are lighthouses in the throbbing ocean of human experience, guiding us towards the shores of communality, tradition, and identity. So, we continue to engage in them sincerely, understanding their essence, appreciating their beauty, cherishing their wisdom, and carrying their flame forward, to light the way for future generations.

Chapter 5. Culinary Chronicles: A Taste of Cultural Heritage

The enchanting aroma of simmering spices, the sizzling noise of preparation in the kitchen, the vibrant hues of an intricately decorated meal - such are the sensorial delights gifted to us by our diverse culinary heritage. Food, a universal necessity, morphs into an art form that generously communicates the richness of diverse cultures, traditions, and histories across the world.

5.1. A Taste of History

The culinary voyage begins with a taste of history - an exploration of the genesis of food as more than nourishment for the body, but also for the soul. Here, we examine the bridges that food production and consumption have built between the mundane and the divine, the everyday rituals and the festive banquets. The primitive human understanding of an edible item as a gift of nature soon evolved. Each culture imbued these ingredients with symbolic meanings, aligning them with their ontology, cosmology, and even anthropology.

From the sacred corn of the Native Americans, the divine wine in ancient Greek rituals, to the symbolic rice in Asian cultures, tangible links are forged between the culinary and the spiritual world. Every meal echoes the footsteps of the past, relishing in age-old familial recipes, forgotten historical upheavals, and epochs of cultural exchange and colonization.

5.2. Global Pantry: Spices, Herbs, and More

Moving on from the historical to the more tangible elements of our culinary chronicles, we delve into the 'Global Pantry.' Here, a robust narrative unwinds about the global exchange and influence that spices, herbs, and staple foods have had in shaping the way people across cultures conceptualize and prepare their meals.

Take the ubiquitous black pepper, the king of spices, for example. Once native to Kerala, a small coastline state in South India, it now holds an indispensable spot in kitchens across the world. Or take the examples of tomatoes and potatoes, both native to America but irreplaceable in Italian and Irish cuisines, respectively.

The story of these spices, herbs, and staples is one of exploration, conquest, trade, and adaptation. It's a tale that shows how organisms from one corner of the earth can travel thousands of miles, spread across continents, merging and mingling with local food habits to create unique culinary traditions.

5.3. Sacred and Profane: The Ritualistic Aspects of Food

Each culture, each tradition, has chosen specific foods and beverages for their symbolic significance, incorporating them into elaborate rituals and ceremonies. This subchapter, 'Sacred and Profane,' captures these foods, beverages, and their associated customs from various cultures.

Consider the Japanese tea ceremony, a choreographic ritual of preparing and serving green tea, imbued with Zen Buddhist philosophies. Or the sacramental bread and wine in Christian communion, symbolizing the body and blood of Christ. The Ethiopian coffee ceremony is another example, where coffee preparation and consumption is an elaborate, hours-long event practiced multiple times a day, serving both as a social gathering and a spiritual experience.

These accounts are just a taste of how food and rituals are intricately entwined in so many cultures. The exploration of such practices appraises the ritualistic aspects of food, bringing us closer to cultural realities and histories.

5.4. Food and Identity: Cuisine as a Cultural Signifier

This section, 'Food and Identity,' provides a closer examination of how food habits, preferences, aversions, and more form a part of personal as well as collective identities. The unique culinary habits and inclinations of a community can say a lot about its history, geography, economy, and values.

In the landscape of cultural gastronomy, some regions are recognized by their staple food, like rice for East Asia, corn for Native Americans, and bread for Europe, while some others might be associated with specific dishes like sushi in Japan or pizza in Italy, each ingredient, each traditional recipe reflecting distinct histories and influences over time.

The exploration of such identities, linked to the culinary habits of people across the globe, unravels the intricate ways in which food serves as more than just sustenance. It tells stories, carries memories, reflects changes, and perpetuates practices sustained across generations.

5.5. The Future of Food Traditions

The final section, 'The Future of Food Traditions,' casts an eye towards the future. It investigates the effects of globalization on food cultures, from the spread of international cuisine to the fusion food trend, while also addressing the urgent issue of sustainability in our food practices.

Food customs, like any other cultural element, are also evolving. As they spread globally, they adapt, absorb and fuse with local food ways, giving rise to novel gastronomical experiences. However, amid these changes, there's also a growing concern about preserving culinary heritage and creating sustainable and equitable food systems. This concern urges us to consider holistic approaches towards our food traditions, taking into account environmental impact, local economies, and social justice.

Unraveling these topics provides an insightful glimpse into the potential trajectories of our culinary heritage, painting a hopeful picture where tradition and innovation harmoniously coexist, contributing to a richer, sustainable, and more inclusive gastronomical future.

In this chapter, we have diced and spiced a cornucopia of culinary traditions, stirring together the ingredients of history, symbolism, identity, and future prospects. Through this journey, every spoonful has revealed the ways in which food - a fundamental human necessity - is intrinsically intertwined with the threads of our global cultural heritage.

Chapter 6. Music and Dance: Rhythms that Bind Us

From the earliest cave paintings depicting men and women moving in synchronized steps around a roaring fire, to the elaborate, passion-filled performances on today's globally acclaimed stages, the association of humans with music and dance has always been an essential part of our cultural tapestry. This relationship is more than recreational; it is expressive, emotional, even spiritual, inextricably woven into the fabric of our civilizational identity. This chapter of our special report charts the enchanting course of these twin threads of our collective heritage - music and dance - as they intertwine across the planet, binding us in a rhythm that transcends borders and resonates with the human spirit universally.

6.1. Echoes of the Ancestors: The Origins and Evolution of Music

Music, as an artistic expression and a means of communication, has its genesis very much rooted at the dawn of human civilization. Predating language, early humans used sounds and rhythmic patterns mimic the melodic contours of nature – the rustle of leaves, the patter of rain, the roaring of a river, the calls of animals - thereby establishing a primal connection to their environment. From the hollowed-out logs and natural skins used to create the first drums, to the carving of bones into flutes, human ingenuity and creative thought bore fruit that would evolve over centuries and across continents into the myriad musical forms we appreciate today.

The development of music as we recognize it today was not an overnight occurrence but an evolutionary process. From the primitive percussive sounds that reverberated in caves, we've journeyed through the choral melodies of ancient Greece, the dramatic orchestras of the Baroque period, the heart-rending arias of the Romantic era, onto the innovative synths of modern pop. Music has grown, transformed and travelled, yet some elements have remained unchanged: rhythm, melody, harmony and timbre - these cornerstones find their echo in every note played, in every song sung, throughout the history of music.

6.2. Dance: The Body Language of the Soul

Parallel to the evolution of music, dance too has traversed an engaging history. Each society, each culture, has its unique dance styles, born of diverse influences ranging from geographic considerations and societal norms to spiritual beliefs and historical events. From the earliest ritualistic dances aimed at appeasing gods and communicating stories, to the elegance of ballet, the vigor of contemporary dance, and the infectious charm of social dances like the salsa or the twist, there is a mesmerizing variety to the dance forms that have sprung up around the world.

The classical dance forms of India, the expressive flamenco of Spain, the graceful hula of Hawaii, the high-energy samba from Brazil or the primal, rhythmic dances of Africa - each narrates a tale, elicits an emotion, speaks a language of the body that deciphers human joys, sorrows, dreams and fears. Dance, like music, is not just a form of entertainment. It is an integral part of our cultural identities, a reflection of society and a tool for unspoken communication that has the power to connect hearts irrespective of linguistic or geographical barriers.

6.3. The Interplay of Music and Dance

Music and dance, in their myriad forms, have often found a common playground where they come together in harmony, creating a synergy that is as enticing as it is powerful. The rhythmic beats and melodious tunes offer a distinct backdrop for the exuberant, emotive, and articulate movements of dance. This intermingling of audio and visual forms of artistic prowess has led to an evolution in globally celebrated art forms such as the opera, the ballet, the musical, even impacting cinema and television.

Whether it's the grandeur of a Viennese waltz set to Johann Strauss II's compositions, the raw energy of hip-hop battles heightened by rhythmic beats, or the intricate story-telling of Bharatanatyam accompanied by the soulful carnatic music - music and dance form an unbreakable pair, each feeding and amplifying the other's impact on the audience.

6.4. Music and Dance: The Rhythms that Bind us Together

In their essence, both music and dance serve as a mirror to the human condition - reflecting our joys, our sorrows, our hopes, our fears - expressing what cannot be put into words. They unite us in our collective experience, dispelling the illusion of separateness. To witness a dance or listen to a melody is to be part of a tradition that has enthralled, entertained and expressed mankind since time immemorial.

In the final analysis, music and dance are not just arts, they are cultural footprints, historical archives, social barometers - and above all, enduring witnesses to the human spirit's intrinsic desire to express, communicate and connect. They encapsulate how we, as a race, have grown, embraced change, held on to roots, and stood the test of time. By engaging with the celebration of this rich and complex cultural heritage, we not only understand the rhythms that have bound us across the ages, but we also join the symphony that reverberates through eternity.

Chapter 7. Customs and Celebrations: Woven Stories of Community

Communities have long been the cradle of customs and celebrations. Their belief systems, histories, environments, and collective aspirations have always served as the canvas upon which the vibrant tapestry of their customs and celebrations are intricately woven. These traditions, which echo the community's spirit and resilience, act as threads that stitch together individuals and generations, giving them an identity, a sense of belongingness, and a continuity of history.

7.1. The Role of Customs and Celebrations in Community

Customs and celebrations encapsulate the essence of a community, distilling their core beliefs, principles, and histories into memorable, experiential nuances. They not only serve as the backbone of a community's cultural identity, but as an indispensable medium through which community values, morals, and stories are passed down from one generation to the next. They lend coherence to the past, imbue meaning to the present, and bestow direction for the future.

Traditions often envelop communal gatherings, fairs, processions, dances, and feasts - often laden with symbolic elements. Every color, rhythm, chant, and morsel of food has its integral role in the narrative. The sense of community is further magnified by participation - unraveling the intricate symbolism and enacting it within the community helps individuals appreciate the significance of their roles.

7.2. Celebrations: A Reflection of Unity in Diversity

Delving into the celebrations around the world showcases our unity in diversity. Each community has its unique way of marking the changing of seasons, births, weddings, harvests, and even remembering those who have passed over with ceremonials and rituals. By celebrating these occasions collectively, communities strengthen their bond. Such celebrations provide a platform where everyone, regardless of their age or social status, can participate and contribute.

Whether it's the vibrant Holi celebrations in India spreading the spirit of togetherness through colors, the Dia de Los Muertos in Mexico honoring their ancestors in unity, or the Panafest in Ghana celebrating African arts, heritage, and unity - all encapsulate the spirit of community. Every celebration, unique in its own right, is a testament to the community's unity, resilience, and communal ethos.

7.3. Customs: The Thread That Binds

Customs are the very threads that bind communities together, giving them a sense of shared history, purpose, and identity. These are not just routine practices or habits but an embodiment of the community's collective wisdom, belief systems, and adaptations over the centuries.

In Japan, the custom of tea ceremonies, or 'Chanoyu', goes beyond the mere act of drinking tea. It's a spiritual journey, an expression of purity, harmony, respect, and tranquility. Customs like the Maori's 'Hongi' in New Zealand, which is an exchange of the 'breath of life' through a pressing of noses, embodies the spirit of sharing, respect, and unity.

7.4. Contemporary Relevance of Customs and Celebrations

Traditions continue to evolve within the context of contemporary society, extending beyond their cultural epicenters. Globalization and cross-cultural exchanges have encouraged the celebration of diverse traditions beyond their origins, promoting cultural inclusivity and mutual respect. For instance, the celebration of Chinese New Year, Cinco De Mayo, and St. Patrick's Day are now observed in many parts of the world, celebrating not just individual communities, but the global human family.

Despite modernization, communities still cling to their traditional customs and celebrations as they serve as a cultural compass guiding individuals and societies. Old customs and rites are recontextualized, given new meaning, and continue to be celebrated to maintain links to their history, their ancestors, and their cultural identity.

In conclusion, customs and celebrations are not just the vestiges of our past. They are dynamic, living entities that evolve with societies, forging communal identities, fostering unity, and promoting mutual respect. As we cherish each celebration and uphold each custom, we weave ourselves into this intricate web of community stories, becoming both the storytellers and the characters within these narratives. This is the essence of the chapter "Customs and Celebrations: Woven Stories of Community."

Chapter 8. Fashion and Identity: The Cloth of Culture

Our voyage begins on a canvas of colors and materials, where personal identity, historical context, and societal norms intersect, crafting a striking visual narrative - the world of traditional and cultural fashion.

8.1. Threads of Identity

Identity, as a concept, encompasses far more than one's personal traits. It is a complex, dynamic, multifaceted prism, reflecting our values, our heritage, and our associations. Fashion, in this light, assumes a profound role, acting not simply as a cloak draping our physical manifestation, but as the fabric of our unique identities, woven from the warp and weft of our varied contexts.

For example, the meticulous embroideries of the traditional Chinese Cheongsam, each stitch painstakingly crafted, tell tales of laborious love and ancient artistry. This garment has become symbolic of feminine grace, cultural pride, and societal transformation in China.

Equally steeped in significance is the Scottish kilt. These unmistakable garments, with their distinctive tartan patterns, do more than just cover - they speak. The different patterns represent Scotland's old clans, translating the wearers' lineage and allegiance into a color palette wrapped around a wearer's waist, essentially turning them into moving, walking emblems of their hereditary ties.

8.2. Clothing: A Socio-Cultural Dialogue

Clothing, deeply entrenched in social systems and structures, has always been playing an essential role in forging cultural dialogues and expressing intricate societal systems.

Take, for instance, the Indian caste system. Traditionally, clothing styles, and even colors, could denote one's caste, thus standing as living embodiments of the complex societal stratification. Dhotis and lungis, for example, were worn predominantly by the lower castes, while sherwanis and achkans, more opulent and embellished, were favored by upper-caste Hindus and Muslim nobles.

Japan's class-conscious Heian period bore witness to the rise of the Junihitoe, a complex twelve-layered robe worn by women of the noble class. Each layer's color and fabric communicated not only the wearer's societal position but subtly hinted at the current season, the time of day, and the immediate occasion, converting the wearer into a silent, visual poet narrating tales of status, nature, and ceremony.

8.3. The Power of Adornments

Adornments and accessories, too, have long been vessels of cultural expression and identity formation. Masai beaded necklaces, Viking brooches, Native American feathered headdresses – they all afford us glimpses into distinct cultures, traditions, and beliefs beyond their aesthetic appeal.

The Maasai tribes of Kenya and Tanzania, for instance, use vibrantly colored beads and intricate designs in their accessories to signify socially relevant information like age, marital status, and even the wearer's mood. The towering feathered headdresses of Native American tribes, on the other hand, represent spiritual connect and honor. Each feather signifies a rite of passage or a feat of valour, transforming these accessories into wearable timelines that encapsulate the wearer's personal narratives and achievements.

8.4. The Influence of Religion

Religion has been a powerful force in defining the fashion landscapes across cultures. The hijab in Islamic cultures acts as an emblem of modesty and spiritual dedication, and the humble dhoti kurta worn by Hindu priests denotes simplicity and piety. Monastic robes in Buddhism, habit in Catholicism, all carry distinct spiritual symbolism and create an unmistakable visual identity.

The breadth of sartorial influences that religion casts on its followers is vast, providing both a sense of unity within the community and a distinct divergence from different faiths.

8.5. Fashion and Cultural Interplay in Modern Times

In recent times, the lines between traditional and modern fashion are blurring, resulting in fusion styles that bring together the best of both worlds. While traditional garbs remain an integral part of ceremonies, celebrations, and rituals, elements of these rich traditions are blending beautifully with contemporary aesthetics, creating hybrid styles that allure and engage across borders.

The Indian sari, for instance, while continuing to be a national favorite, has been playfully experimented with and deconstructed by modern designers, making it a global fashion icon. Similarly, the Japanese Kimono is reappearing in both local and international runways as a fashion-forward, yet culturally anchored ensemble.

The amalgamation of fashion and technology is another fascinating dimension to today's evolving cultural fashionscape. Digitally printed Native American motifs on modern materials, Maasai beadwork patterns transposed onto wearable tech accessories, or interactive textiles that change colors just like mood-ring technology – all signify the exciting intersections of tradition and innovation.

Fashion, by virtue of its visual prowess, bridges the past and the present, the personal and the collective. It is a language that speaks across borders and across time. It is a mirror that reflects our multi-hued identities, and a canvas that lets us paint our stories. As we continue to dress in our identities and narratives, it's intriguing to imagine the fashion landscapes of the future, clothed in the rich tapestry of past traditions and contemporary influences.

Chapter 9. Language Landscapes: Voices of the World

The intricate weavings of human history and culture are inexorably linked to and shaped by one significant element - language. It is our primal means of communication, expression, and understanding. As we traverse the landscape of languages around the world, we necessarily embark on an exploration of the human experience in all its diverse richness.

9.1. The Birth and Evolution of Language

Our journey begins at the dawn of humanity, a time shrouded in mystery and speculation. Although the precise origins of language are lost to us, linguistic scholars posit it may have emerged approximately 100,000 years ago, with the advent of modern Homo Sapiens. Language evolved as a necessity, an indispensable tool for survival and cooperation. Over thousands of years, as humans migrated and settled across the globe, numerous distinct languages evolved, mapping to our species' encounters with varying geographical landscapes and historical events.

Fast-forwarding to present times, there are approximately 7,139 living languages in the world. Each language has its unique construct, grammar rules, and vocabulary size, showcasing the unfoldment of diverse civilizations over time and even hinting at their worldviews, moral values, and cultural nuances.

9.2. The Diverse Tapestry of Languages and Dialects

As we continue our exploration, we encounter dialects, that is, variations of a language peculiar to a specific region or social group. The Cantonese dialect in Chinese or the Scots dialect in English are examples of such variations that add more texture to the linguistic landscape.

Languages and dialects encode cultural knowledge and local wisdom. For instance, the Indigenous peoples of the Americas have hundreds of words for plants, revealing vast knowledge about local flora. In contrast, the Inuit have multiple terms for snow, reflecting their intimate interaction with a cold, icy environment.

9.3. Language as a Tool for Expression and Connection

Besides being a utilitarian tool, language serves a deeper purpose - that of expression, empathy, and connection. It enables the sharing of ideas, stories, and experiences, helping us shape our social identity, relate to others, and build a sense of community. Look at poetry, for example, from the haikus of Japan to the sonnets of Shakespeare. These art forms carved from language inspire deep emotions, painting vivid images of human experiences across cultures and time.

The linguistic diversity also manifests in verbal and non-verbal traditions - from the lively storytelling sessions in West Africa, augmented by drumming and song, to the use of intricate sign languages by communities like the Central Taurus Sign Language community in Turkey.

9.4. Languages at Risk: The Silent Extinction

In contrast to the rich diversity, we find sobering evidence of linguistic extinction. Many languages, particularly those of small, isolated communities, face the threat of disappearing in the face of globalization. Roughly a third of the world's languages have fewer than 1,000 speakers left. The extinction of languages holds within it a loss of cultural diversity, traditional knowledge, and unique worldviews.

Efforts are now underway around the world to preserve endangered languages, from documenting them in extensive databases to developing language instruction programs for the younger generation. The zeal underscores the belief that every language has intrinsic value and cements its speakers to their cultural heritage.

9.5. Language in the Digital Age: New Frontiers of Communication

The digital revolution has significantly influenced the language landscape, offering new modes of communication, from emoji and memes to hashtags and abbreviated lingo. While English is the predominant language on the Internet, the use of other languages is also on the rise, thanks to translation technologies.

Simultaneously, we witness the development of programming languages, artificial intelligence, and machine learning, further expanding the dimensions of the language universe. Herein lies uncharted territories, bearing quotas of profound implications for the future of human communication.

Through this in-depth exploration of language landscapes, the chapter underscores the importance of language in shaping human connection and culture. It highlights the vibrancy of linguistic diversity and the stirring depths of meaning it brings to our existence. The astonishing breadth and depth of world languages, their proliferation, diversification, development, and, in unfortunate instances, extinction, narrate a complex, constantly evolving story of humanity. It is a tale interlaced with trials and triumphs, evolution and extinction, culture and creativity, unity and diversity. And as we stand now on the cusp of a new era, where the digital realm promises to redefine the contours of communication, the tale continues, ever captivating and thought-provoking.

Chapter 10. Religious Rituals: Sacred Traditions across the Globe

Our world is filled with an intriguing array of religious rituals, all reflecting deep-seated beliefs carried through centuries. These sacred traditions take us to the heart of global cultures, giving us a sense of connection to our ancestors' spiritual quests and profoundly shaping the ways in which societies perceive, sympathize, and act. From the plains of sub-Saharan Africa to the bustling streets of India or the serene temples of Japan, we journey through spaces imbued with the divine, showcasing the myriad ways humanity seeks to understand and connect with powers beyond their grasp.

10.1. The Call to Prayer: Islam

Within the Islamic faith, the Adhan is intrinsic, a call to prayer echoing five times daily from the minarets of mosques. Through the words "Allahu Akbar" - God is the greatest - spoken in sonorous tones, the Adhan resounds as a reminder of the Muslim's deep devotion to their religion. Affirming the full faith in the oneness of God and the prophet Muhammad, the hauntingly beautiful prayer call represents the unbroken continuity of a 1400-year-old tradition.

10.2. Lighting the Way: Hinduism

The Aarti ceremony is central to Hindu worship. As the sun sets, worshippers light small lamps filled with ghee or oil in a thali (a platter) and make a clockwise motion in front of the deity's image while singing devotional hymns. The glow from the many wicks in motion create an ethereal sense of peace and connection, bridging the gap between the physical world and the divine. Reminiscent of the cyclicality of life, death, and rebirth, Aarti is a solemn reaffirmation of the devotees' commitment to their faith.

10.3. Connecting with the Ancestors: Indigenous African Religions

In Sub-Saharan Africa, ancestral worship is regarded as an avenue of maintaining ties with departed loved ones. Communities come together to honor the ancestors through elaborate rituals which involve offerings, sacrifices, singing, dancing, and often, divination. These practices bridge the gap between the visible and invisible world, keeping the unending connection between the living and the dead in constant fluidity.

10.4. Sacraments: Christianity

Across Christian denominations are seven sacraments symbolizing significant life transitions. Baptism, Confirmation, and the Eucharist - done as rites of initiation - bring the person into the religious world. Marriage and Holy Orders establish vocational paths towards family or the priesthood. Reconciliation and Last Rites provide solace and absolution, one for the living, and the other for the dying. Regardless of variance across denominations, these rituals give shape and substance to the Christian spiritual journey.

10.5. Tea Ceremony: Buddhism and Shintoism in Japan

Japanese culture, deeply rooted in Shintoism and Buddhism, is renowned for the Cha-no-yu or the formal tea ceremony. Involving disciplined and stylized movements, this meditative practice seeks to cultivate mindfulness, tranquility, and harmony with nature. The meticulously crafted ritual, reflecting aesthetics of 'wabi' and 'sabi,' is a philosophical expression of existence in its transient and imperfect form.

These are but a glimpse into the rich tapestry of religious rituals globally. Though diverse, these traditions reveal a common quest: the human endeavor to understand the dimensions beyond the physical, and the universal yearning to connect with the divine. This yearning has driven humanity across generations and continents, transcending linguistic, cultural, and geographical barriers.

What awaits us beyond this study is a universe of connection and comprehension, ever rich and ever expanding. As we move forward, let us appreciate the authenticity of each ritual, for each carries a piece of our common history, shared values, and collective spirit towards the cosmos. Let us also respect the cultural boundaries and unique values that each tradition upholds. In understanding and empathizing, we nourish our shared human journey and realize the ties that bond us all in the face of divine mysteries.

Chapter 11. Traditions Transformed: The Evolution of Culture in Modern Times

Cultural evolution is an ever-emerging, multi-faceted phenomenon, encompassing changes at both macro and micro levels. It's a dynamic process, a living entity in motion, grappling with modernity, innovation, and globalization, even as it clings to its original roots, creating a complex mashup of the old and new. As global society gallops forward, powered by the omnipresent thrust of technology, cultures around the world are not impervious but are deeply influenced, thus transforming traditions. In this chapter, we delve into the intriguing narrative of cultural evolution, exploring the myriad ways traditions have metamorphosed over time.

11.1. The Changing Face of Traditions

Traditions, by their very nature, carry the nuances of the past, acting as embodiments of communal memory that binds society together. However, in the age of fast-paced globalization, digital communication, and socio-political transitions, traditions are witnessing a perceptible shift. The constant interaction between societies, the sharing of elements between cultures, and the inevitable shifts in sociopolitical landscapes lead to a process of cultural diffusion, adaptation, and hybridization, leading to the creation of neo-traditions.

A poignant example of this cultural shift can be found in the sphere of religious practices. Once an intimate, private domain, these practices have undergone monumental changes with the advent of technology. Today, virtual congregations have emerged as significant spaces for religious discourse and activities, encompassing followers from around the globe in real-time. These digital spaces offer an intriguing blend of old belief structures with new modes of connectivity, reflecting the changing face of traditions.

11.2. The Effect of Globalization and Technology

Globalization and the rapid flux of technology play influential roles in the cultural metamorphosis. Cultural interchange between societies through frequent interaction and exchange of ideas propels tradition transformation. This interchange isn't entirely a new phenomenon, for cultures have always been dynamic and interactive. However, the magnitude and speed of such exchange, facilitated by innovations and modern communication channels, are unprecedented.

Social media platforms exemplify the transformative influence of technology on cultural expressions. Different cultures come together on these virtual platforms, interact, and influence each other. A distinct outcome of this process is the rise of global pop culture, an amalgamation of the traditional and modern, the local and global.

Food culture is another space heavily impacted by globalization. The concept of 'fusion food' combines elements of various culinary traditions, creating new dishes that appeal to a wider demographic. Once region-specific recipes have now traveled across continents, transforming and integrating elements from other cultures along the way.

11.3. Transition in Cultural Identity and Fashion

Traditional clothing is a powerful symbol of cultural identity, reflecting the historical and social nuances of a community. With advancing time, the influence of global fashion trends and the increasingly blurring borders among societies have heralded a significant transformation in traditional attires.

Fashion trends, instrumental in framing societal norms, have seen a paradigm shift. Embracing the global pattern, societies worldwide have integrated elements of modern fashion into their traditional attires, giving birth to a hybrid style. Despite these changes, the significance of traditional attire in marking special events and ceremonies remains deep-rooted, marking the curious co-existence of conservation and transformation in cultural evolution.

11.4. Language Evolution: The Voice of Change

Language, remarkably sensitive to sociocultural and technological changes, serves as a vivid indicator of cultural evolution. With the surge in global connectivity, languages are now in a constant state of flux. New words, phrases, and dialects creep into everyday parlance, enriching and expanding the linguistic repertoire.

English, crowned as the lingua franca of the digital age, has witnessed substantial transformations influenced by Global Englishes, a term encompassing the numerous localized versions of the language. The diffusion of English into non-native environments has led to the development of new jargon, idioms, and accents, reflecting the cultural nuances of the respective regions.

11.5. The Evolution of Art, Music, and Dance

The dynamism of tradition is perfectly captured in the field of art, music, and dance, which have always been sensitive to shifts in societal patterns, climate, and technology.

In music, traditional forms merge with new compositions, giving birth to genres like 'world music,' a creative fusion of elements from disparate cultures. Traditional dance forms, too, have seen an intriguing mix of modern interpretations and traditional movements. Graffiti, once deemed a rebellion form, has evolved into an accepted form of modern art with poignant social and political narratives. These transformations articulate a vivid narrative of cultural adaptation and change—the critical essence of tradition evolution.

11.6. Challenges and Prospects of Tradition Transformation

While cultural evolution creates an exciting blend of diversity and modernity, it also brings along several challenges. The fear of losing traditional practices, language attrition, and cultural assimilation risks underscore the complexity of this transformation process. However, the dynamic nature of culture induces a sense of hope in this situation.

Cultures have showcased a resilient capability to adapt, maintain, and reinvent themselves, despite the odds. Traditions, both old and new, have created a complex, diverse, and rich cultural landscape, mirroring the ceaseless human capacity for innovation and change. The evolution of tradition, therefore, presents a promising prospect of a culturally comprehensive and diverse global community.

As we journey through this transformative era, it is crucial to remain respectful and appreciative of this cultural diversity, enabling traditions to breathe, evolve, and thrive—therein lays the heart of global cultural unity.